Billionaires and Butterfly Ballots

A 20-Year Palm Beach
'Cartoonspective'
By David Willson

Editorial Cartoonist for the
Palm Beach Daily News

2-29-20-FL.

If this were a work of fiction, there would be a disclaimer here that says the characters and events portrayed therein are fictitious, and that any similarities to persons, living or dead, are coincidental and not intended by the author. That is certainly not the case with this book. Every editorial cartoon between these covers was originally created about real people and events, for publication in the *Palm Beach Daily News* during a 20-year span from 1992 - 2012. If you are a Palm Beach public figure and are embarrassed to find yourself inside, then let me take this moment to say: Hey, we all have embarrassing moments. At least yours was entertaining.

Billionaires and Butterfly Ballots
A 20-Year Palm Beach 'Cartoonspective'

www.PalmBeachCartoons.com

ISBN: 978-0-9885365-0-0

First edition: Printed November 2012 by HCI Printing & Publishing, Deerfield Beach, Florida, USA

Billionaires and Butterfly Ballots
A 20-Year Palm Beach 'Cartoonspective'

This family photograph from the late 1800s has appeared in many South Florida history books. It includes Palm Beach pioneers (from left) H. F. Hammond, George W. Lainhart, George Wells Potter, an unknown woman, William Lanehart, Dr. Richard Potter, an unknown child, and Ellen Potter, all posed for posterity. George W. Potter, my great-grandfather, studied art and engineering in Cincinnati before immigrating to Florida with his brother Richard in 1873.

Continuing the legacy

I come from a long line of Palm Beachers, dating all the way back to the island's earliest pioneers. The photograph to the left was taken with a wooden box camera that belonged to my great-grandfather, George W. Potter.

The only thing these early pioneers had in the billions was mosquitoes, but they carved a beautiful little community out of the swamps and gave it the name Palm Beach. All of this happened in the late 1800s, 20 years before Henry Flagler arrived with his railroad and high society.

George W. Potter, an engineer, artist and businessman, drew many of the early survey maps of Palm Beach and West Palm Beach, and illustrated the book *Camping and Cruising in Florida*. After selling his island homestead, he cofounded several businesses in burgeoning West Palm Beach, where he also served as an alderman and mayor.

George married Ella Dimick, the niece of Elisha Newton "Cap" Dimick, who built the first Palm Beach hotel, the Cocoanut Grove House, and served as Palm Beach's first mayor. His statue stands at the entrance to Palm Beach on Royal Palm Way.

Their daughter, Marjorie, married Jack Sloan Willson, a Palm Beach contractor who built many homes designed by Addison Mizner, Maurice Fatio and others. Their son, Jack S. Willson Jr., was my father.

In the '70s, my father developed the Lodge on the Lake, a motel and restaurant complex on Flagler Drive in West Palm Beach. Today, that property is the Trump Towers.

A wealth of local perspective from more than a century of family stories and artifacts has influenced my editorial cartoons for the *Palm Beach Daily News*. In March 1992, when the newspaper decided to add a cartoon to their editorial page each Sunday, I was fortunate to be selected as their first editorial cartoonist. It has been a wonderful relationship and a great opportunity to continue my family's legacy of contributing to the heritage of this community.

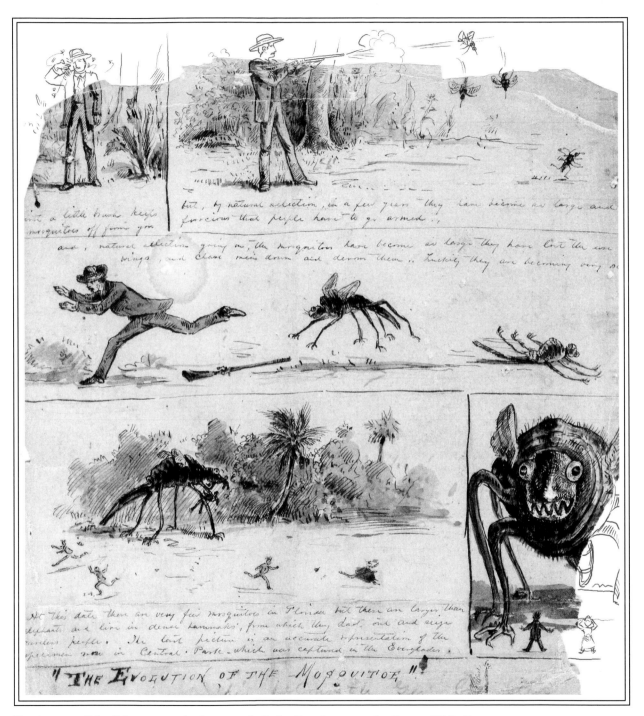

Evolution of the Mosquitoe (sic), *an early Palm Beach cartoon by George Wells Potter.*

This book is dedicated to my father, an architect and businessman who had a cartoonist inside of him clamoring to get out. He would have been my biggest fan, but unfortunately passed away before seeing any of my *Palm Beach Daily News* cartoons. And to my mother, who suffered through years of trying to get me to do my homework when all I wanted to do was draw.

It's also dedicated to my wife Kayla, whose prodigious editing skills and generous commentary have improved many a cartoon and helped provide the illusion that I am literate.

And to the fine editors and writers at the *Palm Beach Daily News*, who I'm sure invite me to editorial board meetings purely for the entertainment value.

And finally, to all Palm Beachers who, time and time again, have proven to be good sports when singled out in a cartoon.

Funny money

Someone once said, "With great wealth comes great responsibility." This may be true, but experience tells us that with great wealth, great excess comes too. Palm Beach is one of those places that accumulates the very wealthy the way the very wealthy accumulate money. They've been flocking here like swallows every winter for more than 100 years, engaging in ritualistic fun and often testing the limits of propriety. Believe me when I tell you that there is no better place for a cartoonist to observe and lampoon the full depth and breadth of human foibles. This 20-year collection is a veritable feast of said foibles. Enjoy.

Billionaires have managed to accumulate a disproportionate amount of the planet's wealth. The irony is that they still have to live on earth with the rest of us.

Around these parts, you often hear the term "Palm Beach rich," as in: "Oh, they've got money, but they're not *Palm Beach rich*." You're not Palm Beach rich unless you can afford a $20 million house, a sport fishing yacht and at least fractional ownership in a private jet without checking your balance. How odd then, that an extra few percent in taxes can send you into a funk.

Very wealthy people are like the rest of us in many respects. Money may be no object, but they still will complain about the food at a banquet.

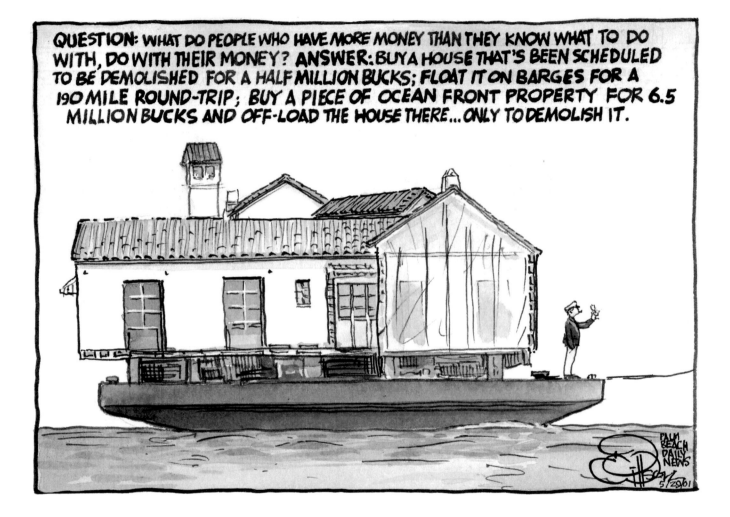

This is a true story.

It's a surprising fact that Palm Beach is not the wealthiest town in America. This is probably because it is a seasonal resort and the trust fund babies, Wall Street bankers and oil magnates in town are merely visitors and not residents — a mere technicality, Palm Beachers will assure you.

The Fanjul family were Cuban sugar growers who immigrated to Florida during Fidel Castro's revolution. They set up shop in the Everglades and are now among Palm Beach's most influential residents. When news broke that a TV series about Cuban sugar barons entitled CANE was in the works, the Fanjuls threatened to sue for invasion of privacy, but then backed off after assurances the show wasn't actually based on them.

Did the previous cartoon just say that filmmakers are not allowed in Palm Beach? Yep, it's true. There is an ordinance against filming in Palm Beach. With a few rare exceptions, feature films have been turned down flat, celebrities have been kicked off the island for filming interviews, and news and documentary crews aren't welcome. I've often thought anthropologists might learn more from observing wealthy Palm Beachers than primitive natives on some remote island.

Given the frequent controversy coming from Rush Limbaugh's Palm Beach radio studio — such as the time he called a college girl testifying before Congress a slut — you'd think the image-conscious town would extend its ban of filming to radio.

NEW NEIGHBORS

Palm Beach used to be considered a wealthy Republican bastion, but things are changing with time.

Here's a great buy! This branch of the royal family inbred themselves
into oblivion by the 1920's ... leaving their Barony available
for just such a lucky couple as yourselves.

Palm Beachers have always been suckers for aristocracy. I mean that literally. There was a booming market in the sale of European aristocratic titles when I first began cartooning for the *Palm Beach Daily News*. Many of these titles weren't worth the sheepskin they were written on, but nobody cared so long as they could write a title like "Prinz von-Schtuppengeld" after their name.

DARN THAT PESKY GUTENBERG!

Why anyone would want to be an aristocrat in today's world, I can't imagine.

Scandals in sandals

He obviously had it in for the citizens of Who'swhoville.

There is no doubt that large sums of money attract scoundrels and lead some people into temptation. Enough of it, and you start thinking you can buy your way out of just about any situation. Palm Beach may be a laid-back tropical setting, but its history is so full of cautionary tales that it reads like Aesop's Fables. You might say my cartoons are the illustrated version.

Congratulations Roxanne

Peter and Roxanne Pulitzer's divorce was the scandal to beat all scandals. In a lurid trial, Peter Pulitzer succeeded in convincing a judge to award him custody of the kids and let him keep most of his money by recounting a long list of his wife's threesomes, affairs and drug use. But Roxanne got her revenge by writing tell-all books and doing a Playboy photo feature depicting every incident made famous by the trial, including some eye-popping stuff with a trumpet. When Roxanne remarried seven years later, I was happy to send her on her way with this cartoon.

I barely missed covering the Willie Kennedy Smith trial, because it concluded just weeks before I began cartooning for the *Palm Beach Daily News*. Still, it left a lasting legacy in Palm Beach that the Kennedys never got over. John F. Kennedy visited the family house in Palm Beach so often during his presidency that people referred to it as the Winter White House. But after it later became the scene of the Willie Kennedy Smith's date rape scandal, it was often besieged by the press and paparazzi.

DADS, NOW THAT WE'VE HAD OUR OFFICIAL COMING OUT, WE'VE DECIDED WE WANT TO STAY OUT... AT AU BAR TONIGHT!

Willie Kennedy Smith's troubles began during a Boys' Night Out with Uncle Teddy and Cousin Patrick at Au Bar, an infamous nightspot where hook-ups were the main attraction. Au Bar was the island's den of iniquity, following a tradition begun by E. R. Bradley's Beach Club during the historic Flagler era. Such establishments have always been the Yin to Palm Beach society's Yang.

OH NO, NOT ANOTHER TRUMPISM! I'M GOING TO FAIL THIS COURSE!

Donald Trump has the distinction of having had two highly sensational Palm Beach divorces — the first after Ivana caught him canoodling with Marla Maples in Aspen, and the second after police found Marla canoodling with a Trump bodyguard on the beach. As we all know, Mr. Trump is quite adept at dealing with difficult circumstances and bad press. This can lead to some interesting headlines and unusual conundrums.

THE MEDIA HAS DEPICTED ME AS A BOUNCER LIVING WITH A STRIPPER...
THEY'LL TWIST ANYTHING TO SUIT THEIR OWN PURPOSE!

Stephen Fagan kidnapped his little girls after losing custody in a Massachusetts divorce. He changed his identity with a stolen Social Security number and hightailed it for Florida in 1979. Fagan eventually married a rich Palm Beach widow, and by the time he was arrested in 1998, was thoroughly ensconced in Palm Beach social and philanthropic circles, promoting himself as an ex-CIA agent, founder of a think tank and former presidential advisor. He picked the right place to pull this charade. To this day, there are still Palm Beachers who insist he is an upstanding guy.

Millionaire murderer Fred Keller treated Palm Beach to not one, but two highly sensational trials. One for shooting and killing his ex-wife and badly wounding her brother in (you guessed it) a divorce settlement meeting, and the other to straighten out all the claims against his estate after he died of cancer in jail. The preposterous proceedings featured codicils to his will from competing attorneys for the victim's family and his heirs. Even his cellmate got in on the act, presenting a handwritten document stating that Keller left everything to him — just to spite everyone.

Jeffrey Epstein had a knack for making lots of money and very important friends. He lived the ultimate jet-set billionaire's lifestyle. Unfortunately, he wasn't able to keep his kink for underage girls in check and was arrested. A dream team of attorneys managed to wheel and deal Epstein out of all but one charge for soliciting prostitution. A plea deal netted him an 18-month prison sentence, of which he served 13 months. Most of that time was spent in his private office on work release under the supervision of a sheriff's guard that he paid for. Once released, he became Florida's first jet-set parolee.

NEW TABLOID FODDER: CONVICTED PEDOPHILE JEFFREY EPSTEIN IS PRINCE ANDREW'S GOOD FRIEND WHO PAID OFF FERGIE'S DEBTS.

Once word of Epstein's penchant for massages from high school girls got out, poor Prince Andrew was in hot water again. The tabloid press discovered that Epstein had been paying off some of the Prince's ex-wife Fergie's debts. Andrew had even stayed at Epstein's Manhattan crib and was photographed socializing with an underage masseuse. The scandal eventually cost the Prince his official title of Special Envoy for Commerce and got him ostracized from public royal events.

Polo mogul John Goodman ran a stop sign on his way home from a day and night of partying. He broadsided and killed Scott Wilson, a college student driving home from school. This was a tough one for me to cover, because Wilson was the son of a guy I often sat next to in high school. Goodman's A-list lawyers cooked up a heady brew of farfetched mitigating excuses, including one that he lost control of his Bentley because the accelerator stuck. When Goodman was finally convicted, it occurred to me that the unrepentant multimillionaire would finally learn what losing control is all about.

Colorful Palm Beachers

EASTER 1959: AN AUSPICIOUS MOMENT IN PALM BEACH HISTORY

Palm Beach has had its bounders and floozies, but tropical island life, by its very nature, is more conducive to affability. I bet after his divorce from Roxanne, Peter Pulitzer wished he had stuck with earlier wife Lilly. By founding the Lilly Pulitzer fashion empire, Lilly defined Palm Beach's laid-back image with bright Easter egg colors.

Billionaire Bill Koch treated Palm Beachers to an entirely self-funded Western memorabilia exhibit in early 2012. He filled four exhibition halls to the rafters with Western and Native American artifacts, antique guns, giant gold nuggets, an entire saloon, stagecoaches, rare photographs and priceless paintings. The Smithsonian would be envious, but for him it's a hobby. This was only a portion of his entire collection, which will eventually be housed in a completely restored Colorado ghost town, just for family and friends to play in. Now *that's* Palm Beach rich.

CHANGES IN LATITUDE

When the world's most famous barefoot troubadour moved to Palm Beach, I thought it was pretty funny. I mean, very few flip-flops are blown out on Worth Avenue. On the other hand, I can see what may have attracted Buffett to this town. Palm Beach may be more opulent than Margaritaville, but it's still a tranquil paradise.

*MEMORABLE LINE FROM THE BESTSELLER *LIFEGUARD* BY JAMES PATTERSON AND ANDREW GROSS.

Leave it to Palm Beach's best-selling author to capture in one sentence how high society blends with our mellow tropical climate.

Island survival skills

Despite being surrounded with luxurious trappings, Palm Beachers often face peculiar challenges. There's always a humbling happenstance waiting around the corner. At times, it seems like the local gods have a hidden agenda to teach the wealthy and privileged a life lesson about humility.

"THE BRIDGES OF PALM BEACH COUNTY"

She saw him across the water. He looked at her and waved. His lean muscles rippled, echoing his reflection in the lake beneath. She waved; and wondered at the unfairness of life. He was so close, yet two bridge construction projects, 12 miles and a 45-minute detour away.

PALM
BEACH
DAILY
NEWS
6/11/95

Palm Beachers have always had to contend with bridge closings due to maintenance or reconstruction. The town of Palm Beach is on a barrier island, connected to the mainland by three bridges. It is surprising how many times two of the bridges have been closed simultaneously. This 1995 cartoon used the popular film, "Bridges of Madison County" to poke a little fun at such exasperating circumstances.

THE FLORIDA STATE DEPARTMENT OF TRANSPORTATION - WHERE TWO WRONGS DO MAKE A RIGHT.

The Florida Department of Transportation is responsible for most of these snafus. They have a funny idea of what the word "scheduling" means.

Palm Beach probably has one of the highest Ferrari per capita ratios in the nation. But that's nothing compared to the speeding ticket per Ferrari ratio.

Lifestyles Of The Rich And Furious

Airport noise is something that even the wealthy have to endure in Palm Beach. Palm Beach International Airport, situated in the middle of West Palm Beach, is only 2.5 miles from some of the most expensive real estate in the world.

Of course, an airport within a couple of miles of Palm Beach has its advantages for presidential candidates who like to take the money and run.

Parking is at a premium on a small island. For many years, the Palm Beach parking patrol marked tires with chalk to ensure that parking spaces were vacated in a timely fashion. Palm Beach also happens to be a turtle nesting area in the summertime, which gave me the idea for this cartoon about how it's not always possible to complete your business on such a strict schedule.

For new residents, life in Palm Beach can be much like a cutthroat game with a steep learning curve.

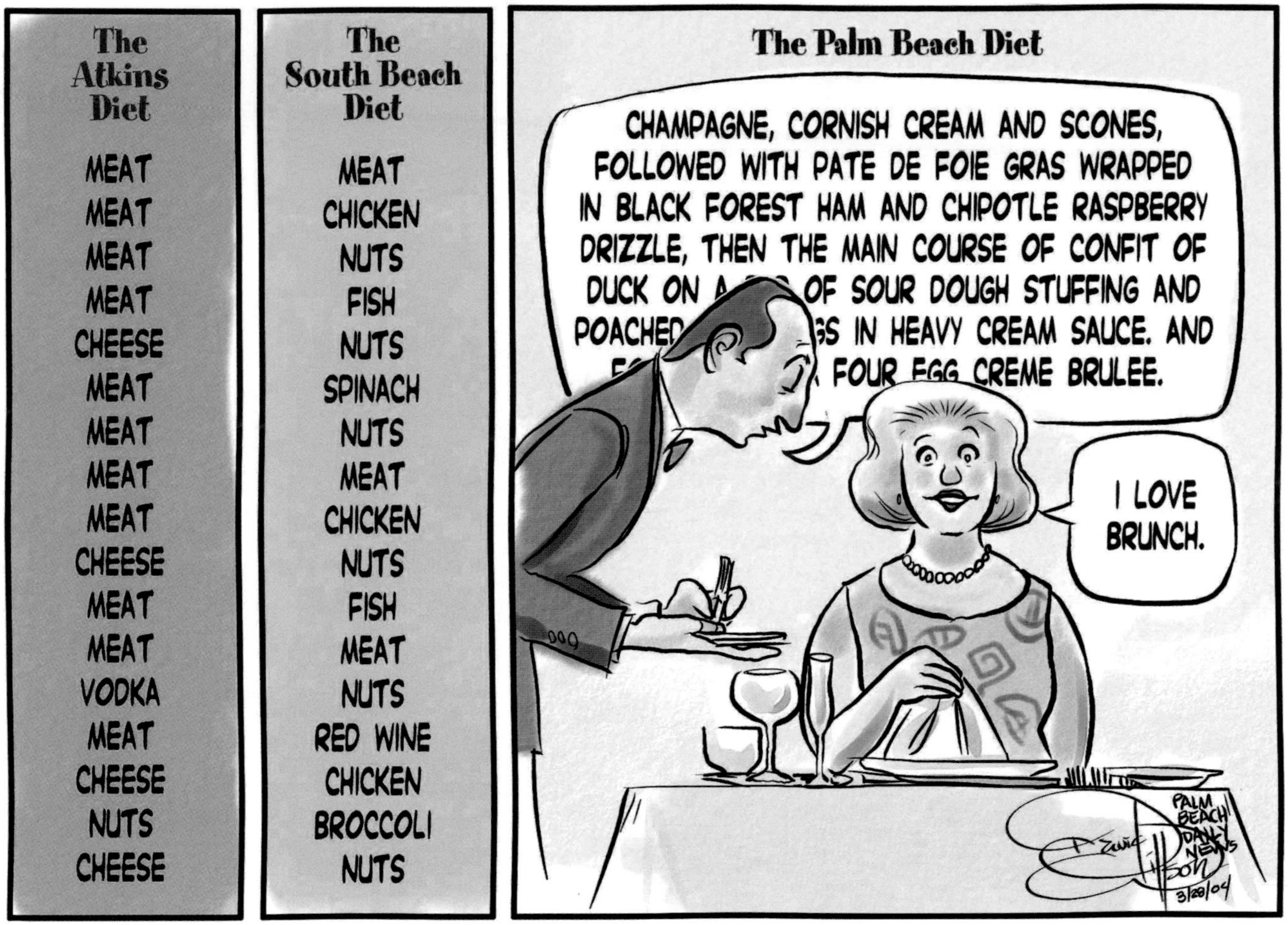

Sometimes, too much of a good thing can be a challenge too.

The Palm Beach social season can be daunting for a well-connected islander.

Dodging hurricanes

Palm Beach has been relatively lucky and has experienced only a couple of disastrous hurricanes in its history, but this cartoon pretty accurately describes how we feel about the buggers.

The National Hurricane Center's five category system for describing hurricane strength and potential damage can be confusing. So, I decided to do a version that most Palm Beachers could relate to.

A FEW WEEKS AGO HE WAS ALL-POWERFUL. NOW HE'S JUST DEPRESSED.

It doesn't matter how omnipotent you are in the boardroom — going through a hurricane is a frightening and humbling experience. This cartoon was done after Hurricane Francis skirted the Palm Beach area in 2004.

THE HURRICANE GODS RUN THE TABLE.

2004 was a year when the odds were not stacked in our favor. Four storms hit Florida. Two of them, Francis and Jeanne, made landfall three weeks apart in almost exactly the same spot, just north of the Palm Beaches.

HURRICANE SEASON MEETS PALM BEACH SOCIAL SEASON.

Hurricane Wilma blew through at the end of October 2005. Full-fledged hurricanes are almost unheard of in the late fall. It's a time when we typically have some of our most delightful weather and the first snowbirds start making their way down for the social season. Surprise!

Insurance companies pulled out of Florida en masse after Hurricane Andrew, claiming that their funds were insufficient to cover losses from another similar storm. Never mind the outstanding profits they enjoyed during decades of light hurricane activity. The Florida legislature's solution was to form its own windstorm insurance pool, as an insurer of last resort. But starting from scratch, they required outrageous premium payments.

Shocks felt around the world

Whether you were a fan of John F. Kennedy's presidency or not made little difference when little John John saluted his father's casket on national TV. He became America's son at that point. Ironically, JFK Jr. would grow up to launch a magazine named after the father of our country. And then, he was gone.

REALITY SHOW

We were just getting used to the new phenomenon of reality TV when one earth-shattering event brought us back to reality.

The unified anger in America after the 9/11 attacks was so palpable that I could only imagine what Osama bin Laden was thinking when he realized he'd aroused the sleeping giant, just like the Japanese did with Pearl Harbor.

WELL, IT LOOKS LIKE WE'LL HAVE THE BEACH TO OURSELVES THIS SEASON.

Within a month of the 9/11 attacks, news broke of an anthrax outbreak at the American Media office building in Boca Raton. Air travel had already plummeted as a result of the hijackings. Not a good year for Florida tourism.

HALLOWEEN 2001

If anthrax could be distributed in the mail, what were the possibilities of tainted candy or an aerosol dispersal during Halloween? Suddenly, the holiday got scary for real.

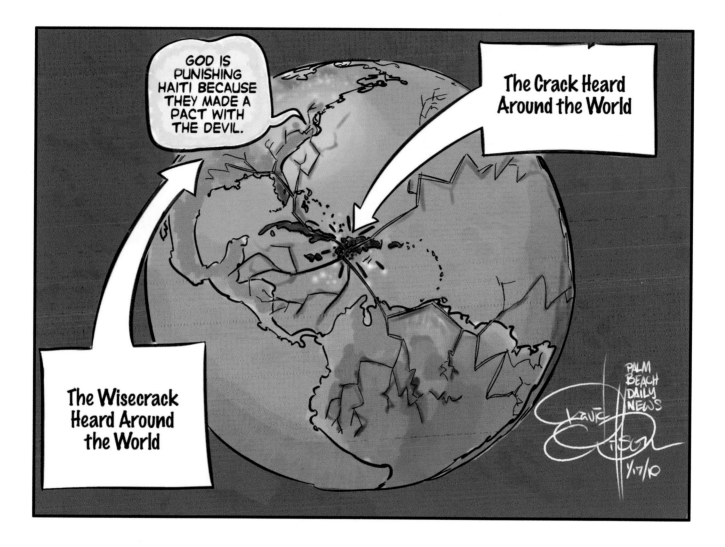

The Haitian earthquake was bad enough. Horrible. But then it takes a crackpot like Pat Robertson to make it worse.

There are natural disasters, and then there are man-made disasters. The outcomes can be very similar, but the difference is clear.

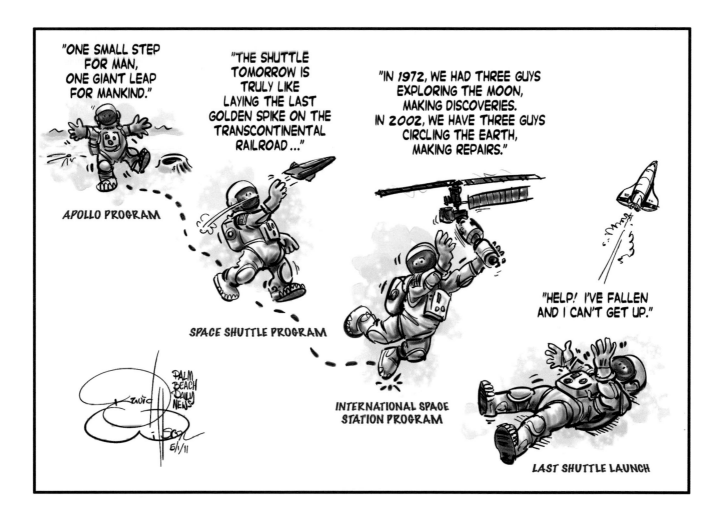

I had a toy Cape Canaveral launching set when I was a kid. The Mercury and Gemini programs were the backdrop to my elementary and middle school years. Neil Armstrong walked on the moon right after I graduated high school, but then *this* listless trajectory began. Can you imagine a more inauspicious way for government to end the first decade of a new millennium?

Nature gone wild

Although the mosquito-infested swamps of my ancestors are long gone and people now outnumber the pesky bloodsuckers, increased travel and world commerce have introduced some rare mosquito-borne diseases that still warrant distinctly unfashionable precautions.

FORMER EXOTIC PETS ARE SHOWING UP EVERYWHERE.

Being labeled exotic in Palm Beach just means you're more fashionable. Exotic has a whole other connotation if you are a python or a boa constrictor. These non-native predators were released in the Everglades by pet owners who could no longer care for them, and they began wreaking havoc on the local ecosystem. If only their owners had released them in Palm Beach.

IGUANAS GONE BAD IN MANALAPAN

Iguanas, another pet gone wild, were pooping in swimming pools, deflowering gardens, and generally making a nuisance of themselves in the tiny enclave of Manalapan. Shockingly, hundreds of the cold-blooded lizards met their demise the following winter, when record cold temperatures had them dropping out of trees.

FIRST SOCIAL EVENT OF THE SUMMER SEASON...

THE MEMORIAL DAY BEACH DANCE

No one really understands why we started getting Sea Lice (jellyfish larvae) infestations in the surf along east coast Florida beaches. The microscopic critters were unknown when I was a kid. But today, many ocean swimmers end up doing a frantic dance for a few weeks in May, at the start of every summer.

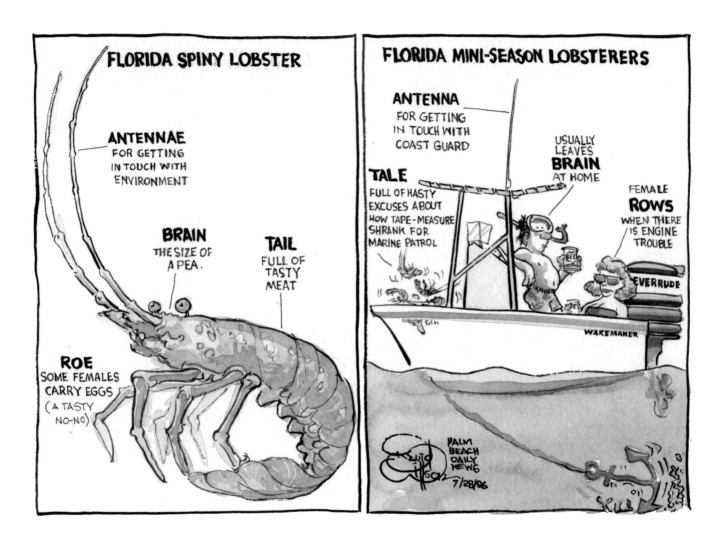

Florida lobsters are tasty, but they resemble a giant aquatic insect more than anything else. Still, they are a highly evolved species compared to some of the human beings involved in the annual mad melee of Florida lobster mini-season.

I have no doubt that much of Palm Beach island will swim with the fishes someday. It's only a matter of time. Environmental activists seem intent on hastening that day. While I sympathize with protecting natural reef habitats, it's getting more and more difficult for South Palm Beach air breathers along the most eroded section of coastline, Reach 8, to keep their condos from falling into the sea.

Feral cats and pampered pets

Legend has it that Henry Morrison Flagler imported cats on the island in the early 1900s to keep the rat population down at his Royal Poinciana Hotel. Palm Beach has had feral cat colonies ever since. This has created endless political and social strife. Initially, residents and businesses, including the Flagler Museum, were having them trapped and removed, but this never seemed to diminish the population.

Animal rights proponents insisted that the correct approach was to capture, neuter and return cats to a well-fed colony. Cats are very territorial, so the non-breeding cats would control their colony's size by keeping interlopers out. The town did not see it this way, so cat feeders faced fines and even arrest if caught. Instead of cat burglars, local authorities were on the lookout for cat wranglers.

FERAL CHIC

Eventually, the Palm Beach Town Council was convinced that the controlled colony tactic was really the best way to go, so they authorized a group of volunteers who were permitted to feed and maintain neutered colonies. Feral cats were officially invited into the Palm Beach social order.

The town of South Palm Beach, which is primarily comprised of oceanfront condos, decided to crack down on feral cats and their feeders. Many people wondered why they didn't follow the same new approach taken by neighboring Palm Beach. But I knew. The cats must have run afoul of a condo restriction.

COMPARING FERAL CAT PROGRAMS

The town's backing of PB Cats has been half-hearted at best, with minimal financial commitment. The resulting program was so poorly funded that it paled in comparison to other programs. Even the scruffy, laid-back Florida Keys had us beat.

But after all, what would you expect from people who tend to see themselves as aristocrats?

Palm Beachers love their pets, and they have plenty of money and time to lavish on them. Every one of the examples depicted in this cartoon are common occurrences around here.

Still, pet owners face an entrenched culture of NIMBYism in Palm Beach. It's hard to find a park where walking your dog is allowed. Every time one is proposed, the neighbors become a howling pack of naysayers.

But the town of Palm Beach is generally a dog-friendly environment. Dogs are even allowed at outdoor seating of many of its restaurants.

Cats, not so much. This cartoon ran the week after the one on the previous page.

Like most other towns, Palm Beach has ordinances that address people who love pets a little too much. Former Palm Beach gallery owner James Hunt Barker (no kidding) had to take his 16 spaniels and move where such rules don't exist.

The saga of Piggie Pie Freckles, the Vietnamese pot-bellied pig, ran concurrently with that of Martin Millar, mayor of South Palm Beach. Piggie Pie, a Palm Beach pet pig, riled neighbors with constant scuffling and rooting noises. Millar riled bouncers in a strip club by providing his own spotlight service with a flashlight. Both were subsequently ostracized for their piggish behavior.

Social dyslexia

Pets often receive better treatment than people in Palm Beach — outsider people that is. Some Palm Beachers have a conniption at the idea of outsiders crossing the bridges to visit the beach or go shopping. This attitude has found its way into the town government over the last 40 years, resulting in reduced parking spaces, a dearth of public restrooms, and a "town-serving" ordinance that forces restaurant and shop owners to provide an audit proving that more than 50 percent of their customers live on the island.

CONDO MENTALITY = SOCIAL DYSLEXIA

When I was a kid, the Palm Beach public beach had a fishing pier, oceanfront shops, swimming pools and plenty of parking for everyone. But in the mid-1960s, property owners sold the shops and pools to condo developers. When the pier was damaged by a hurricane and had to be removed, some stairways to the beach mysteriously disappeared. Parking was reduced and concrete scallops were put on the seawall to discourage sitting. Today a visitor can easily drive by the area without realizing that it is still a public beach.

Though Palm Beach is chartered by the state of Florida like any other town, some residents prefer to think of it as a gated community. Yes, the Palm Beach Town Council has literally entertained proposals to put guard gates on all the bridges.

THE SCARIEST THING ON WORTH AVENUE THIS HALLOWEEN.

The town-serving troops invariably gather to protest any new business that looks like it might attract outsider customers. Popular restaurant and retail chains need not apply. There was even vocal resistance when ultra-luxury retailer Neiman Marcus announced its intention to build a store on Worth Avenue, simply because it was a department store.

Believe it or not, these are actual quotes from a Palm Beach town council member when a West Palm Beach-based water taxi service proposed a landing at the Flagler Museum. In reality, the landing made perfect sense, because water taxis were the main source of transportation to and from the mainland during Flagler's era.

The town decided to erect a statue of Henry Flagler at the north bridge entrance to Palm Beach. The bridge was first built to convey private railcars of wealthy seasonal guests to Flagler's Royal Poinciana Hotel. Today, however, Palm Beach's original main street is a hotbed for anti-development, anti-condo and anti-everything naysayers, who seem intent on stopping any vibrant revitalization.

It's important to remember that people who have their noses up in the air about town-serving businesses are in the minority. This has been substantiated by Palm Beach Chamber of Commerce business surveys. I have seldom come in contact with a true snob in Palm Beach because they prefer to congregate at exclusive Palm Beach clubs with restrictive membership policies.

The Sailfish Club, primarily a fishing and yachting club, was always one of the least prejudicial toward new members and guests. However, due to the fact that they lease shoreline for their docks from the state of Florida, they were required by law to include non-discriminatory membership language in their club's charter. The private club's board thought they were being unfairly singled out and refused to comply, only to have their docks condemned by the state.

After a year-long and much publicized battle, the Sailfish Club finally relented and changed their charter to officially open membership to all races and creeds. That doesn't mean that attitudes changed elsewhere on the island. Not too long afterward, a Palm Beach policewoman pulled a gun on a black man waiting in his car to pick his wife up from work, saying he looked like a gang member.

Perhaps taking a cue from the Sailfish Club brouhaha, Donald Trump promoted his new Mar-a-Lago Club as a less stodgy alternative to other Palm Beach clubs. The new general manager stated emphatically that all types of people were welcome, so long as they could afford it.

Donald does Palm Beach

In 1985, Donald Trump bought the town's most iconic mansion, Mar-a-Lago, saving it from the wrecking ball. When he later ran into financial difficulties, Trump managed to hold onto the property by turning part of it into a prestigious club. By saving the iconic estate, Trump did Palm Beach a very big favor, but he's had to fight town hall every step of the way. They love nothing better than to say, "Donald Trump, you're fined!"

The very first cartoon I did about Trump was actually about Ivana, which makes sense because after their divorce she was totally out to steal his press.

IVANA- PALM BEACH'S FIRST TABLOID COLUMNIST

Eminently qualified, Ivana took a job at *The Globe* tabloid as an advice columnist to the lovelorn.

Henry Flagler let nothing stand in his way as he aggressively pushed his railroad through Florida. Similarly, Donald Trump advanced many of his local enterprises by threatening massive lawsuits against antagonistic town and county governments. They invariably backed down and gave him huge concessions. Flagler and Trump have had their detractors, but you can't argue with the results.

Trump's Mar-a-Lago Club has been the scene of many cartoon-worthy events. For instance, right after Trump purchased the Miss Universe pageant, the first crowned beauty began putting on weight. As a new owner, he publicly took on an unusual new role and seemed to be channeling Richard Simmons. I might have gotten carried away with the comparison, because the caricature looks more like Simmons — only with Trump's hair.

Minnesota governor and former wrestler Jesse Ventura tagged Trump as a possible presidential candidate for the 2000 Reform Party ticket. In a flurry of media appearances, Trump made noises like he was ready to jump in the ring. But Reform Party founder Ross Perot was not happy with Ventura or Trump, so he backed former Republican candidate Pat Buchanan, and Trump said enough is enough.

Trump revisited the idea of running for president in 2011. He was interviewed on every network and cable channel in a media blitz that was reminiscent of his exploratory campaign 10 years earlier. But with all of the overlapping multimedia exposure today, his limited focus on China and OPEC grew monotonous fast. Interestingly, he started adding new material shortly after this cartoon ran. I wonder … coincidence?

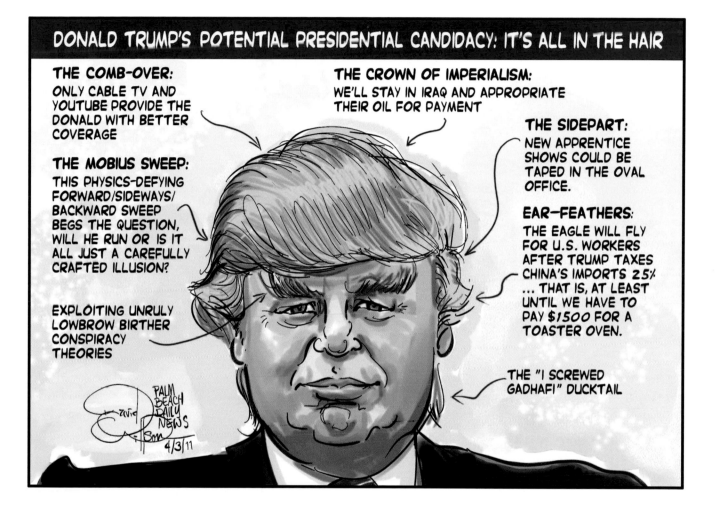

I suppose my advertising background was responsible for this cartoon. When you have a strong brand symbol, it's a good idea to tailor your message in terms of that memorable image.

The elusive butterfly of politics

FLORIDA IS OVERRUN WITH LITI-GATORS

As a native, my take on the 2000 election brouhaha in Palm Beach County was a bit different than that of other editorial cartoonists around the country. Instead of participating in partisan bickering over the close results, I was appalled by the invasion of nearly a thousand carpetbagging attorneys from both parties dead set on deciding the election in the courts. I felt this was a dangerous precedent that might change American politics forever. In hindsight, I think I was right. The parties have a litigious strategy for every election now.

The media went on a feeding frenzy as soon as it got wind that some Palm Beach County voters thought they might have mistakenly voted for Pat Buchanan instead of Al Gore on what became known as the Butterfly Ballot. Other states had worse snafus, but those results weren't as critical to the outcome of the election, so the focus was on Florida. We ended up being portrayed in much the same manner as a Third World country that can't be trusted to oversee its own election.

After both sides fought tooth and nail all the way to the Supreme Court, nearly derailing the orderly transition of government, President-elect George W. Bush called for the country to come together and heal.

During the year following the 2000 election, Palm Beach and Dade Counties' ballots became the most recounted and analyzed in history. In the process, it was discovered that a Palm Beach County woman had registered her dog to vote — and we were back on *Letterman* again.

Naturally, the media floated Florida out as a hobgoblin before the next presidential election in 2004 ...

... not that it really mattered, considering the level of political discourse that year.

It has now become standard practice to file a lawsuit when results are close. So it's no surprise that judges have come under increasing political pressure. A political campaign is being waged to unseat three Florida Supreme Court justices as I write. This has forced the justices to raise campaign funds for their defense. Now I ask you, when it comes to maintaining judicial impartiality, do we really want judges to be seeking big financial donors?

One need only refer back to an earlier cartoon I did during the O. J. Simpson murder trial to see how unhealthy litigating more elections would be. Those with unlimited funds can hire a Dream Team to chip away at legal procedures until they get the desired outcome, making it a much more attractive approach than elections to affect change in government.

The notable illustrator and cartoonist James Montgomery Flagg popularized Uncle Sam with his famous "I WANT YOU" poster for World War I. Flagg did several illustrated posters about Americans coming together for the common good. I've often wondered what he and his generation would think of us today.

Congress obviously is guilty of many of the same foibles as ordinary Americans. What they don't seem to understand is that we expect more from them.

Another fine(ancial) mess

ALAN GREENSPAN, FATHER OF OUR ECONOMY

Alan Greenspan made a preemptive strike against inflation early in 2000, raising interest rates. This had an immediate effect on the stock market. Given his penchant for making blunt statements in front of Congress, this seemed like the perfect metaphor.

Fraudulent accounting practices came to light in the down market following the 2000 tech crash. Companies like Enron, Adelphia, Tyco and WorldCom could no longer keep a lid on deceptive accounting practices and illegal insider loans. Consequently, the Sarbanes-Oxley Act was very quickly enacted, and thousands of public companies restated their financial documents over the next few years.

Penny stock firms were regulated out of business and the brokerage industry consolidated. Many of these firms were located in Palm Beach County. I wondered if out-of-work stockbrokers went back to the jobs they'd held before being recruited and trained to pitch stocks over the phone — you know: selling paint, delivering pizza, waiting on tables.

Lately, bad financial news seems to hit around Halloween time, and the tricks have kept on coming despite tons of treats.

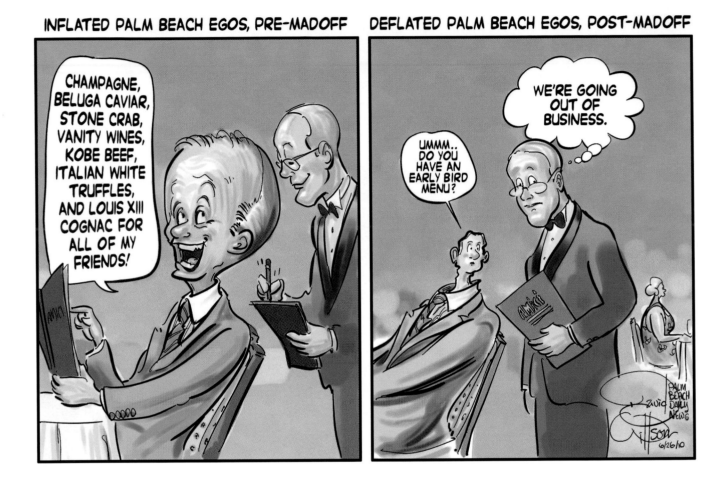

Palm Beach was hit particularly hard by the Madoff Investment Securities fraud, and businesses that catered to conspicuous wealth soon found wealth conspicuously absent.

SEASON'S GREEDINGS

The Madoff ponzi scheme was the largest investment fraud in U.S. history, but only one of numerous such schemes uncovered by the global recession. After a year of revelations about plundered pensions, robo-signed foreclosures, investment scams, governmental cronyism and nefarious banking practices, the 2009 holiday season was not so jolly.

Community commotions

CAREER STUDENT

If anything ever gets done in Palm Beach, it's usually after a great deal of time and money has been spent on studies. Residents are still waiting for the Town Council to graduate.

By Jove, Akhmed! I believe we've just discovered that the ancient pyramids were built because of a zoning compromise that called for increased setback requirements on upper stories!!

Layers upon layers of zoning have been applied to various neighborhoods over the years, sometimes with unintended results.

Town politicians like to compare the Palm Beach Town Council to a New England caucus style government. Sometimes it seems more like a Transylvanian lynch mob.

HYSTERICAL PRESERVATION

All plans for renovation or new construction must be reviewed by at least one of several commissions dedicated to preserving the town's charming ambience. Unfortunately, buildings must be designated historic landmarks before they can be protected against demolition. Many new residents think bigger and newer is better, so the town has fought a losing battle to save some very unique buildings.

Ultimately, the town's preoccupation with zoning ordinances has little effect, because the Town Council will hear any request for a variance and frequently approves them.

THE SCARIEST THING IN PALM BEACH THIS HALLOWEEN

The problem with citizen politicians in a highly social environment like Palm Beach is that there is little incentive to make tough or unpopular decisions. Those issues tend to drag out, unresolved, for years. The Town Council eventually made necessary cuts to police and fire pensions, but the process was so slow and rancorous that employee morale was severely affected.

Unlike Palm Beach, West Palm Beach adopted a strong mayor system and elected Nancy Graham in 1991. She took the strong mayor moniker literally, which was not good news for Palm Beach when the end of a 99-year water contract approached.

Palm Beach and West Palm Beach have two main medical centers. The non-sectarian hospital, Good Samaritan, got into financial difficulties in 1994 and was taken over by the Catholic management of the other medical center, St. Mary's. Suddenly, certain elective surgery procedures disappeared from the Palm Beaches. Ultimately, they relented under public pressure.

For some reason, as soon as arts organizations in our area start having success — be it ballet troupe, theater, opera, or artists' collective — they always start looking to own a building, build a facility or even get involved with mixed-use real estate development. Invariably, they lose focus of their real artistic purpose, and that's the end of their success.

Half the town of Palm Beach heads back North during the summer. During that time, there is very little happening down here for the *Palm Beach Daily News* to cover. In fact, it is not uncommon for the paper to run articles and photo spreads about events in Saratoga or the Hamptons — and for me to do cartoons like this.

A New Year's tradition

As the millennium approached, we were all on edge. Some people thought that airliners would fall from the sky and life would descend into apocalyptic chaos due to the millennium bug, a computer time clock programming glitch. Everyone breathed a sigh of relief when nothing of the sort occurred. This cartoon started me on a path of using the old man and baby motif to address the overarching themes of each year.

DON'T LAUGH, SOMETHING TELLS ME I'M GOING TO NEED ALL THE MAGIC I CAN GET.

With the 9/11 and anthrax attacks, 2001 was a frightening and disturbing year. Coincidentally, the blockbuster dark fantasy films released that year were perfectly matched to our mood.

Chasing al-Qaeda in Afghanistan was one thing, but by the end of 2002 it was clear we were preparing to invade Iraq, and future generations would have to deal with the consequences of expanded and protracted war.

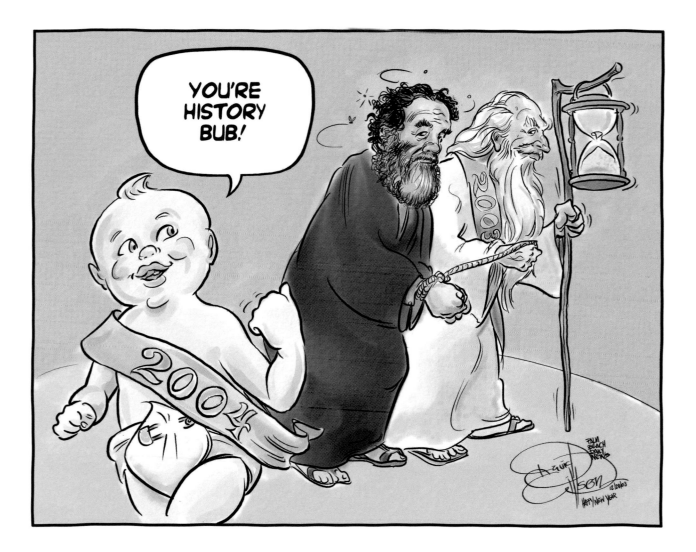

We celebrated Saddam Hussein's relegation to the history books in 2003. He was a despotic dictator who deserved everything he got. Although, it seems like a hollow victory when you look back on it now.

Hurricanes Wilma and Katrina hit Florida and the Gulf Coast with devastating results in 2005. New Orleans was flooded when its decrepit levee system failed. But the big story that emerged by the end of the year was how poorly equipped and unprepared FEMA was.

In 2008, it seemed like we went from Change to spare change in a heartbeat.

We spent most of the first decade of the new millennium trying to ignore the fact that the world economy is a house of cards. By 2010, one ponzie scheme after another was surfacing, and just about everything was up for auction. It was a buyers' market with no buyers.

In today's world, Attention Deficit Disorder is probably not a disorder. It's the norm.

I keep hoping that someday everyone will finally get fed up and deal with the real culprits.